Things couldn't be more normal in Tim Sample's Maine. Hubie's up to his usual cockamamy projects — teaching his dog to talk, inventing boneless chicken — Mother is still driving a truck, and Unc, up to Eastport, is holding forth with the snappiest one liners east of Cutler. But, as lovers of the best-selling SATURDAY NIGHT AT MOODY'S DINER know, normal to Tim ain't what it seems to most folks!

POSTCARDS FROM MAINE is the latest installment from the mind and pen of Tim Sample, who **Yankee** calls, "Maine's premier humorist-story-teller." Like one of those packages of postcards you can buy on Route One, POSTCARDS FROM MAINE contains ten classic stories: some new, some not so new, but all punctuated with Tim's unique blend of traditional Maine humor in a contemporary style. Illustrated with **loads** of drawings, Tim believes you don't have to be from Maine to appreciate the book. But it helps!

So, enjoy this little journey into Tim Sample's Maine. And when you're done, send POSTCARDS FROM MAINE to a friend out of state — maybe they'll stay there!

Tim Sample is native. He lives in Bath and wants to hear from you. Perhaps you will drop him a line requesting all the stuff he can't sell out on the highway. Go ahead, write him!

Sample Studio
16 Winter Street
Bath, Maine 04530

Postcards from Maine

Also by Tim Sample

Illustrator

How to Talk Yankee (with Gerald Lewis)
Stories Told in the Kitchen (with Kendall Morse)
Aunt Shaw's Pet Jug
Hoskin's Cow

Author & Illustrator

Saturday Night at Moody's Diner
Postcards from Maine

Postcards from Maine

Stories and Drawings by Tim Sample

Tilbury House, Publishers
Gardiner, Maine

Copyright © 1988 by Tim Sample

Some of the contents of this book is derived from material originally recorded on *Downeast Standup* and *Back In Spite of Popular Demand*,   ·
produced and distributed by Bert & I Records, Ipswich, Massachusetts. The author and publisher gratefully acknowledge the use of this material.

Library of Congress Catalog Card Number: 88-80185
ISBN: 0-88448-050-X

Designed on Crummett Mountain by Edith Allard
Composition by Lettersystems, Inc., Hallowell, Maine
Printing & Binding by Arcata Graphics

Manufactured in the United States of America
THIRD PRINTING

Tilbury House, Publishers
The Boston Building
132 Water Street
Gardiner, Maine 04345

For Patty Sample

My wife, my partner, my very best friend

Special thanks to: Capt. Kendall Morse and Joe Perham for some valuable "insider trading," R. Valentine Gray for professional encouragement throughout the project, and of course, Edith Allard, without her talent and perseverance this book would not have been possible.

Contents

Postcards from Maine

Introduction

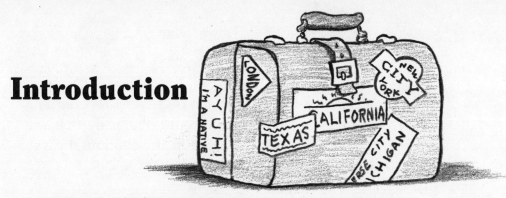

"How's things goin', Tim?" The question came from a familiar voice behind the counter of the Early Bird Market in Winslow, Maine.

"Awright, I guess," I said. "Too busy, that's all. Just got back from Colorado, now I got to spend about a week workin' on this film I'm doin' down on the coast, then I'm off to some place called Traverse City, Michigan, for a one nighter. With the airlines the way they've been this summer, there's no tellin' where I'll end up or when."

Connie's head popped up from behind the counter where she'd been sorting returnable bottles. "Well," she said, "it does sound like you're pretty busy. I just got one question for y', Tim."

"What's that?" I muttered.

"I was just wonderin'," she replied with a little smile, "are you braggin' or complainin'?"

Of course I had to laugh. And of course Connie was dead-on in her assessment of my situation. She wasn't trying to be mean. Her snappy one-liner simply captured the essence of downeast wit and wisdom and its gentle good humor.

I'm often asked by New Englanders whether people outside our region really get my stories. The question always brings to mind a series of posters I saw as a boy in the subway on my first trip to New York City. Each one featured a face grinning from ear to ear and munching a big slice of delicious looking dark bread. All races, creeds, colors, and ages, happily munching that bread. The caption on each read "YOU DON'T HAVE TO BE JEWISH TO LOVE LEVY'S RYE BREAD!" And obviously that was true. The part that wasn't written in the caption always sounded in my brain a few seconds later — "BUT IT HELPS!" That was also true!

So you don't have to be from Maine or even New England to get this stuff. But it helps! I guess I'd say you don't have to come from Missouri to get Mark Twain or from Oklahoma to get Will Rogers...but it helps!

Whether you're from around here or from away, I hope you'll enjoy this little journey into the world of Maine humor. Whatever you do, don't take anything you find between these covers too seriously. I believe that humor is the great lubricant of the human spirit, and if I can apply a little oil where you need it, I'll consider the whole endeavor worthwhile.

Set 'er Again

Set 'er Again

Bert and I was haddock fishin' this one particular summer. As I recall, the fishin' itself wunt all that good, but the weather was warm and sunny, which made fishin' a lot more appealin' than wadin' through a swarm of summer folks in town. So all in all we was havin' a pretty nice summer.

Along about the first of August, however, I noticed Bert actin' mighty peculiar. For more than a week he'd been arrivin' at the dock at the crack of dawn, happy as a clam in the mud and just burstin' at the seams with enthusiasm to go fishin'.

Anybody who knew Bert could tell right off that that kind of behavior at that hour in the mornin' just wunt like him. Not that he was bad tempered or anything. Just sort of a slow starter. Normally the first hour or so in the mornin' he just drug himself around, mumblin' and bumpin' into stuff. By the time we'd loaded the bait and the gear aboard and I'd poured a half dozen cups of black coffee into him, he'd be talkin' in whole sentences. And by the time we got out to where we was gonna be fishin', he was passable good company.

But as I say, along about the first of August I seen a whole new side of Bert. When I pulled up at the dock he'd be there already loadin' the gear and whistlin' a tune chipper as a jaybird. After a few more days of this I couldn't stand it any more, and I begun to question Bert. After a little backin' and fillin' he finally admitted that the reason he was so happy to spend all his time fishin' was that his mother-in-law was visitin'. That cleared up the mystery in short order.

Now don't get me wrong. I've got nothin' against mothers-in-law as a general category. I'm sure there's plenty of great ones out there, and I'm a firm believer in the old adage "Behind every successful man there's a surprised mother-in-law." But the fact remains that I've met Bert's mother-in-law on several occasions, and I wouldn't wish her on my worst enemy, let alone my best friend.

To start with, this woman has got to be one of the largest creatures that ever walked God's green earth. She ain't just large, she's positively massive. Now I'd be the first to admit a preference for large women. I've always said a heavyset girl is shade in the summer and warmth in the winter. But that mother-in-law of Bert's has carried a good thing too far. Plus, in addition to her overpowerin' physical bulk, she's got a capacity for verbalization that would put them fast-talkin' TV evangelists to shame. That woman could talk the varnish off a canoe paddle before she really warmed to the conversation. Needless to say, I sympathized with Bert's dilemma.

6

On the last day of her visit, Bert was in rare form.
I'da never thought a man could whistle, hum, and grin all
at the same time, but I swear he was doin' just that when
I arrived at the dock about 5:30 in the mornin'. "Great
day fer fishin', ain't it?" he bellowed as he tossed the bait
barrel aboard. "I dunno," I muttered, "ain't been up long
enough to notice." By this time Bert's jubilant spirit had
started to wear on me a mite.

7

I cranked the engine a couple of turns, and she fired up and settled into her familiar coughin' and a-chuggin'. Bert cast off the bow line and the stern line, and he was just about to loose the springer line when I heard an ungodly wail outta him. Sounded for all the world like a cow stuck in a barbed-wire fence. I glanced up in the direction he was lookin', and I seen it, too. It was an awesome sight.

Sure enough, it was her. No mistakin' it. A great huge Cadillac with Massachusetts plates was barrelin' down the dirt road headin' straight for the dock. There was a cloud of dust spewin' out behind, and all the shock absorbers on the driver's side was shot to hell. She screeched to a halt just short of the dock, and through the dust cloud I could make out that great beefy arm of hers wavin' frantically out the window. Then I heard her bellowin' through the settlin' gravel. She was bound and determined she was goin' fishin' with us.

We knew right off we was trapped, and there wunt nothin' we could do about it. Bert heaved a sigh and made the lines fast. We headed up the ramp and made our way to the driver's door. Bert opened the door and we pryed her out; then he got on one end of her and I got on the other, and somehow we maneuvered her down the ramp to the float. 'Course all this time she was talkin' a blue streak. Anybody with enough sense to leave the scene already had. Even the seagulls had hightailed it outta there.

Somehow we loaded her aboard, centered her as best we could, and made our way out of the harbor towards open water. It was a nice mornin' weatherwise. The inner harbor was glassy calm with just a bit of sea smoke risin' off the surface. If anything, the tranquility of the scene

8

spurred her on to greater levels of oratory, and she drowned out the engine without half tryin'.

But a funny thing happened as we approached the mouth of the bay. We begun to strike just a mite of heavy water. Nothin' serious, you understand, just a reg'lar five- or six-foot rollin' swell. As soon as we hit them swells, I noticed a change in our passenger. Her monologue definitely dropped several notches in volume. Bein' an old deepwater man, I took this as a sign, and sure enough, she begun to look a little green around the gills, and it

wunt more than five minutes later she was up over the gunnels with an awful load o' chum. I could tell right then and there it was gonna be a long day.

By the time we'd anchored and started in to fishin', Bert's mother-in-law was feelin' mighty poorly. We laid her down in the bilge in order to make her more comfortable, and she settled into a reg'lar pattern of more or less sloshin' and moanin'. As the swells rocked the boat from side to side, she'd slosh almost up to the port gunnel. Then as the wave passed beneath our keel, she'd drift back to starboard and let out this low moanin' sound kinda like a barn door creakin' on a damp mornin'.

Back and forth she went, a-sloshin' and a-moanin' at reg'lar intervals. To tell the truth, compared to the yackin' she'd put up earlier in the voyage, that sound was almost soothin'. It was almost like that music they play down t' the K-Mart, just kinda background stuff that's real easy to ignore.

Meanwhile, Bert and I was havin' the best fishin' we'd had in quite a spell. On account of bein' so preoccupied with the fishin', I can't honestly say exactly what happened next. But apparently this wave come along that was just a little bit bigger than the rest of 'em. 'Course that's not unusual when you're a few miles out to sea. Well, I guess that wave musta smuck us a good whack along the starboard beam just as Bert's mother-in-law was on the upslosh to port. The only thing I can say for sure is that all to once she went sailin' over the side like the *Spruce Goose*, smacked the water with a thunderin' wallop, and proceeded straight to the bottom, slick as a cup o' custard.

I was surprised! I'da thought someone with that girth woulda had a certain amount of built-in flotation. No sir!

10

Down she went just like a stone, and it was obvious the minute it happened that there wunt a darn thing we could do about it. So we kept on fishin'.

Towards the end of the afternoon we hauled in the gear and headed for port. We made the mouth of the harbor just about twilight, stowed the gear in the boathouse, brung the boat out to the mooring, rowed the tender back to the dock, and then Bert, of course, run right off to call his wife and break the news. 'Course she was mighty upset about the whole thing — anybody would be! — but we explained there wunt nothin' we coulda done about it.

As you might imagine, the next few days was pretty hectic over to Bert's place. The family arrived from all over. Then realizin' there wunt nothin' to be done up our way, they all drifted back down to Massachusetts, where a few days later they held a memorial service for the dear departed. On account of the circumstances of her depar-

11

ture there was no need to order a casket; prob'ly a considerable savings to the family right there.

I suppose the whole thing was pretty tough on the family, but fortunately life goes on. A couple of weeks later the whole incident had pretty well blowed over and things was gettin' back to normal. Bert and I was down to the fisherman's co-op one Friday mornin' about 5:00. I was finishin' my second cup of coffee and Bert was over in the corner playin' the Pac Man machine when Richard Wall, one of the local lobstermen, come over and started in with a little friendly banter.

"You remember that heavyset girl you boys had out fishin' with y' a couple weeks back?" he says.

"Ayuh," I replied.

"Well," he went on, "I just thought I'd let y' know she washed up on the beach down to Mill Cove last night."

"Y' don't say!"

"Ayuh, musta been the same one. 'Bout the size of a pilot whale?"

"That's her all right," I muttered. "What kinda shape was she in?"

"Not too shabby," he said, "considerin' where she's been and all. I will say she had almost two dozen good-sized lobsters clingin' to 'er."

"Y' don't say," I replied.

"Ayuh," said Richard. "Most of 'em 'd run two pounds or better."

I thanked him for the information and went across the room to break the news to Bert.

"Godfrey" he exclaimed, lookin' visibly upset. "They've already had the service and everything. What am I gonna do now?"

"Look, Bert," I said. "I realize this is kinda touchy. It's really a family matter, and I prob'ly ought to stay out of it altogether. But things bein' as they are, what with the state of the economy and the price of lobsters and so forth... Well, my advice would be *set 'er again!"*

Teddy Roosevelt
Visits Greenville

Teddy Roosevelt Visits Greenville

Nobody would ever accuse Greenville, Maine of bein' a bustling center of cultural activity. But over the years this little village has attracted a mighty impressive list of national politicians, business tycoons, and well-known sports and entertainment celebritites. What brings 'em to Greenville? Good question.

The founding fathers of Greenville plunked their town right smack dab on the shores of Moosehead Lake and just around the corner from Squaw Mountain. Whether it was the hand of divine providence, dumb luck, or more likely a little of each that drew the original settlers, it turned out to be a darned good move. You see, it didn't take long for word to get out that if you were lookin' for the best huntin' and fishin' in the state of Maine, you

17

need look no further than Greenville. Moosehead Lake
seemed to overflow with record-breaking togue and
salmon, and the surrounding woodlands were chock full
of bear, moose, deer, and other game animals large and
small. Yes sir, Greenville was a genuine sportsman's
paradise.

By the turn of the century Greenville was geared up
in fine shape to handle the surge of city-slicker "sports."
Huntin' camps, sportin' goods stores, and local guides
were almost as thick as the black flies. One of them stores
was run by Nathan "Gramp" Shaw, a fixture in the town
and well known to locals and sports alike. For the better
part of 90 years he'd been offerin' unsolicited advice and
commentary from behind the old brass cash register at
Shaw's General Store.

Gramp Shaw had what folks back in them days refer-
red to as a "contrary nature." If a particular point of view

was held by the majority of Greenville residents, that was reason enough for Gramp to take the opposite tack. Most everybody complained about his thickheaded positions on everything from the best black-fly repellent to local politics and world commerce, but few if any of 'em would argue the fact that Gramp's ideas added a dollop of spice to the constantly bubblin' conversational stew around the store's potbelly stove on long winter afternoons.

Now true to form, at a time when rural Maine was made up almost entirely of dyed-in-the-wool Republicans, Gramp Shaw was about the only registered Democrat in Piscataquis County. Nobody who knew him could possibly have expected otherwise. The year was 1904 and the ol' Rough Rider himself, Teddy Roosevelt, was runnin' for president, second time around on the Republican ticket. Folks in Greenville was foursqaure behind old T.R. Not only was he a solid Republican, he was a well-known hunter, fisherman, and all-round sportsman to boot. Since Teddy had set up camp in the White House it seemed like all kinds of folks across America had caught the huntin', fishin', and campin' fever. As a result, a whole lot of shoe salesmen and postal clerks from places like Paramus, New Jersey, found their way to the camps around Greenville to follow the lead of the chief executive. No doubt about it, Teddy Roosevelt was darned good for the local economy.

So you can imagine the excitement that swept the village when they found out the president himself was comin' to visit. Word was that Teddy was takin' a weekend off from the pressures of the campaign trail to do some fishin' on Moosehead Lake.

The whole thing come about kinda sudden, but the town responded with unbridled enthusiasm just the

same. By the time the presidential Pullman arrived at Greenville station early the following Friday, there was a sizable contingent of local dignitaries on hand to welcome the president and his entourage. The train depot was decked out with red, white, and blue bunting, and the remnants of the 20th Maine Regiment blew a passable rendition of "Hail to the Chief" as the president's car pulled to a shuddering halt at the platform. "Pug" Pinkham, head of the local grange, delivered a welcomin' address along with a key to the village and an invitation to speak at the grange hall that Sunday evening.

Gramp Shaw had enough gumption to miss the festivities at the depot, but even he couldn't resist the temptation to attend the grange hall meeting. Come Sunday night the old barnlike structure was packed to the rafters a good two hours in advance of the president's appearance. It was a warm August night, and the black flies and mosquitoes were jockeyin' for prime position. Kids swung their legs from the rafters overhead as pudgy ladies fanned themselves in the wooden folding chairs.

When the president arrived not a soul was disappointed. Teddy Roosevelt strode onto the stage at the stroke of 8:00 with a brand of self-confidence rarely glimpsed in that sleepy village. Ladies swooned and men applauded with gusto. From the first sentence it was obvious that the citizens of Greenville were enthralled.

All but one citizen, that is. As the masses cheered, Gramp Shaw slumped deeper and deeper into his folding chair and glowered and snorted at the speaker, obviously not impressed by his oratory.

Midway through the second hour of his talk, President Roosevelt fully appreciated the mood of his audience. He was preachin' to the faithful, so t' speak,

21

and he knew he could do no wrong. Flushed with his success, he committed a fatal error.

"How many of you out in this crowd tonight are registered Republicans?" he roared. The response was overwhelming. Every hand in that jam-packed hall rocketed skyward. Every hand, that is, but one. Gramp Shaw sat in the back row with his hands tucked neatly underneath his armpits and fixed the podium with a withering stare.

Now a lot of public speakers would have taken the crest of the wave and kept on goin', but this Roosevelt fella was one to take on a challenge. He noticed right away that there was only one dissenter in the crowd, and then and there he decided to tackle him.

"My good man," the president began, "would you mind standing up for a moment?" He said this in a tone that drew chuckles from the audience, virtually all of whom were aware of Gramps' political persuasion.

"Don't mind if I do!" countered Gramp, leaping defiantly to his feet to face the great man.

Roosevelt continued, "Would you mind explaining to me how it is that in an area so heavily Republican as this, you happen to be the only Democrat?"

"Well, replied Gramp, "that's pretty easy to figure. My daddy was a good Democrat, and his daddy before him. So likewise I'm a good Democrat."

"Well," says Roosevelt, not missin' a beat, "I suppose if your father and grandfather had been jackasses, you'd be a jackass, too!" The audience howled with laughter 'til the rafters rang with the echo of it. It had taken the president of the United States to do the job, but somebody had finally taken the wind out of Gramp Shaw's sails.

But Gramp wasn't quite finished. He kept up his steely-eyed glare, then a grin began to form at the corners of his mouth. His reply came slowly, accompanied by a twinkle in his old gray eyes. "No, sir, Mr. President," he replied. "In that case I guess I woulda been a Republican."

The Continuing Saga of Our Boy Hubert

The Continuing Saga of Our Boy Hubert

Some of you folks might already know about our boy Hubert. For any of you who don't, a little explanation is prob'ly in order.

Hubert lives out behind our trailer in a 1958 DeSoto sedan. He's got the car inside the barn to keep it out of the weather. When I mentioned to him that the barn roof leaks pretty bad, he said it was all right on accounta the car roof leaks a lot worse. He's numb as a hake, but he *is* good with his hands. You heard of folks that don't know nothin'? Well, I'm afraid Hubert don't even *suspect* nothin'. But he's a good-natured boy and surprisingly clever in his own way. It's just that his mind is constructed on a highly original floor plan.

One thing I will say for Hubert, the boy is just full of ideas. If you think about it, most folks come up with ridiculous ideas on a pretty reg'lar basis. You know the kinda thing I'm talkin' about, like why don't somebody invent a radio for pickup trucks that only plays country music? Foolish stuff like that comes poppin' into your head all the time, right? The only difference is that when you and I think of some crazy idea like that, we toss it right away the next minute 'cause we see it for what it is, a useless numb idea. Hubert, on the other hand, takes ideas like that and bangs away at the cussed things for weeks tryin' to jump start 'em into reality.

Surprisingly, every now and then one of Hubie's ideas actually does some real positive good in the world. So don't get the wrong idea about Hubert. He may be numb as a hake, but he's a good boy just the same.

Hubert Gets His Deer

Here in Maine, deer huntin'
season takes up most of November
and has developed into an annual
ritual of staggerin' proportions. For a few weeks every fall,
the whole state goes through such a weird transition it's
downright spooky. All of a sudden, almost like one of
them old "Twilight Zone" episodes, everyone mysteriously
disappears and you find yourself walkin' through a ghost
town.

From the first day of deer season to last, the normal
activities of day-to-day life come to a screechin' halt.
Wanna get yer car tuned up? Sorry, mechanic's gone
huntin'. How 'bout a haircut? Nope, barber's huntin', too.
Who's that new fella stumblin' through the weather report
on TV? Oh yeah, 'course. The reg'lar weatherman is off
huntin'. Tryin' to get that new garage built before the
snow flies? Forget it, Bub. For the next few weeks them

29

bright yellow bulldozers and backhoes 'll be standin'
around in the sun like a bunch of dinosaurs at a
museum. The contractor, foreman, and rest of the crew
are all off huntin'.

'Course our boy Hubert is just as eager as the rest of
'em to test his skill against the elusive white tail. The fact
that all Hubert generally gets is a ragin' head cold and
frostbit toes don't dampen his enthusiasm one bit. If that
boy was to go deer huntin' 300 days in a row and come
back empty-handed every day, he'd still be convinced that
next mornin' out he was gonna get that big buck. I'll say
this much for Hubert. He may be number than a
pounded thumb, but he ain't no quitter.

This year as openin' day approached, Hubert was more excited than ever. He was real eager to try out the new equipment he'd been workin' on. His latest brainstorm was a set of electrified long underwear he'd whipped up from an old pair of my long johns and about 40 feet of that heat tape you wrap around pipes to keep 'em from bustin' in the winter.

He'd also figured out how to attach his binoculars to the underside of the visor on his safety-orange huntin' cap. It was a pretty straightforward arrangement involvin' about a half pound of duct tape. The trouble was that once they was strapped onto the visor, them binoculars (a WWII surplus pair that musta weighed a good 10 pounds) tended to pull the whole hat frontwards over Hubert's face. The result was that instead of gettin' a better view of his quarry, he couldn't see nothin' at all. 'Course, as always, Hubert had a solution. He figured since he needed electricity to run the electric underwear anyway, he'd find a battery about the same weight as them binoculars and hook it onto the back side of his hat as a counterbalance. As it turned out, he pirated one off an old busted snowmobile he was savin' out in the barn. It was just the right size and heft for the job, and he rigged up a cradle for it outta old coat hangers. Once he'd snagged the ends of the coat hangers through the back side of the hat and hooked up the terminals to the heat tape in his long johns, he was ready for action.

By the time Hubert was outfitted in his new gear, he looked a whole lot more like somethin' out of *Popular Mechanics* than the L.L. Bean catalog. But he was wicked excited about tryin' out the stuff, and there wunt the slightest doubt in his mind that this'd be the year he got that big buck. As I watched him headin' out the door grinnin' ear to ear, with that Ski-Doo battery bouncin' off the back of his neck, I wondered for the two thousandth time why Mother and I had ever decided to have kids.

We didn't see hide nor hair of Hubert for the next three days. We wasn't worried, though. God in his infinite wisdom seems to take special care of folks like Hubert. No matter what happens to him, he always seems to end up all right. About midnight on the third day I heard the blown muffler on the old pickup chug into the driveway, and I knew Hubert was home.

The next minute he come burstin' in the front door wavin' his arms like some wild Indian, jumpin' up and down, and yellin' for me and Mother to quick come outside right away. "I got me a deer!" he hollered at the top of his lungs. "It's a big one too! Daddy, come quick! I shot me a great big buck with a 12-point rack!"

As I put on my robe and slippers and dug out the flashlight from the dresser drawer, I couldn't help but be a little skeptical of Hubert's claim. Not that he ain't truthful, you understand. He just tends to get even more muddled than usual when he's aggitated. Last year Hubert was huntin' with Edith Fowler when she got her a deer. Hubert run right home and announced Edith'd got herself an 11-point buck. When I finally saw the critter for myself, it turned out that Hubie's idea of an 11-point rack looked like this.

As Mother and I made our way out the front door, Hubert kept on hollerin'. "Daddy," he says, "guess what?" (With Hubert there's no point in guessin'. In the first place you'd never even come close, and in the second place he's gonna tell you within two seconds anyhow.) "I killed that deer with just one shot outta my rifle!" Now I'll admit that that statement really got my curiosity goin'.

When we got outside, the pickup was parked in the driveway, and to my surprise there was a great cruncher of a buck deer layin' in the bed. That deer was so heavy the springs was squished flat and so big the whole front half of 'im flopped over the tailgate. Despite my original skepticism, I'll have to admit I was some old impressed. But I still had one question about the whole situation.

When Hubert'd come babblin' into the house a few minutes back, I definitely heard him braggin' how he killed that deer with just one shot. First of all, Hubert's rifle is a K-Mart special that prob'ly cost him all of $50.00, and it's about as accurate as the Bangor weather forecast, which is to say not very. On top o' that, even an expert marksman with top-notch equipment ain't likely to drop an animal of that size with one shot. So I took my time and looked over the carcass pretty close.

No doubt about it, there was a bullet hole right between the eyes that mighta been enough to do the critter in. But as I looked a little closer, I noticed that the right front leg was mangled up pretty good, too. It looked suspiciously like a bullet hole. So I begun to question Hubert. "Son," I said, "I don't mean to cast any doubts on yer story or anything like that, but I thought you told me you killed this deer with one shot. If that's so, how'd his leg get shot up like this?"

Hubert just stared at me lookin' kinda shocked, like I'd hurt his feelin's real bad. "Daddy," he says, "I swear it's nothin' but the God's honest truth! It's just that when I shined that flashlight in his eyes, he went like this!"

Hubert's Drink 'n Drive

Lately, as you prob'ly know, there's been hot and heavy debate in Maine and the rest of the country over the topic of folks drinkin' and drivin'. First there was this group called itself Mothers Against Drunk Drivers, MADD. Next come the young folks with Students Against Drunk Drivers, SADD. Then it wunt long before I started seein' these bumper stickers for DAMM, Drunks Against Mad Mothers. All of a sudden we had quite a storm brewin' over the issue.

As anyone livin' in Maine for the past few years can tell you, "Maine has a *tough* drunk driving law!" The folks down to Augusta passed the law a few years back, and they've been plasterin' that slogan all up and down the highways and on radio and TV ever since. You'd 've had to have been passed out cold on the sofa for a few years to have missed the message.

Now Hubert heard the message same's we all did, but he thought of somethin' that never dawned on sharper minds than his. "Sure," he thought, "Maine's got a tough drunk drivin' law, all right. But Maine's also got a grand old tradition of drinkin' and drivin'!" 'Course he was absolutely correct.

I don't mean for a minute to imply that Maine is full of drunks or drunk drivers. What I will point out is that Mainers are real protective about their social customs, and just passin' a law about this or that don't mean a whole lot to folks who feel they've got a God-given right to be doin' whatever it was a law was passed against. If a law comes along that interferes with what a native feels is his or her right to do things the way they been doin' 'em for generations, the law pretty much gets ignored. That might seem like a fine point to some. But Hubert saw the possibilities right off and started in on a solution to the problem.

He begun with the notion that Mainers' are darn well gonna drink and drive no matter what law gets passed. A six-pack of beer might as well be standard equipment on

every pickup sold in the state. And a smelt shanty or a
huntin' camp is considered uninhabitable without a good
stock of hooch.

On the other hand, Hubert's as concerned as the next
person about the idea of good honest folks and innocent
bystanders gettin' bunged up or even outright killed by
mixin' alcohol and gasoline. So he begun workin' on a
plan to preserve Maine tradition and save lives at the
same time.

First thing Hubert done was to rent the Newport
gravel pit for New Year's Eve. Everybody knows that's
prob'ly the prime time of the whole year for drunk drivin'.
Once he'd made the arrangements with the selectmen, he
set about refurbishin' the place. I've got to hand it to
Hubert. He really got his hands dirty on that project.
After about a week of workin' dawn til dusk, he brung
Mother and me over to let us glimpse the fruits of his
labors.

We was mighty impressed. Hubert had transformed
the gravel pit into a darn good likeness of a typical Maine
road. He had 'er decorated with them wooden silhouettes
of fat ladies bendin' over. He'd erected fake phone poles
with little safety-orange frost-heave signs on 'em. He'd
even built a full-size plywood trailer cutout, three or four
shades of pink and green and complete with tires on the
roof, a TV in the bay window, and a healthy scatterin' of
lawn ornaments in the front yard.

Next he set to work paintin' a great big red, white,
and blue sign which, after gettin' permission, of course,
he erected on Elmira Dodge's front lawn out on Route 2.
The sign had a big arrow pointin' the way into the pit
and was lit up with multicolored flashin' Christmas lights.
In big blue letters about two feet high, the sign read

HUBERT'S DRINK 'N DRIVE
OPEN 24 HOURS
EVERYONE WELCOME!!!
GRAND OPENING NEW YEAR'S EVE!!

Hubert took out ads in the local papers and put up posters everywhere from the bowlin' alley to the Baptist church. The idea was this. You'd drive down to the gravel pit on New Year's Eve (reservations recommended) and pay Hubert $15.00 per person. That fee would entitle you to half an hour at the pit in our old Dodge power-wagon pickup and a free six-pack of Narragansett or Colt 45 for the driver and each passenger. Just the beer and the gas to run the big old V-8 in the pickup would pretty much be worth the admission price.

For a full half hour folks could ram around the gravel pit at breakneck speeds hootin', hollerin', and gettin' drunk as a skunk. You could smack into stuff, back up, and smack it again if you wanted to, all the time guzzlin' beer and heavin' the cans out the window just like you would on the highway. Everybody could have a grand time doin' what they was plannin' on doin' anyway. When yer half hour was up, Hubert would make sure someone drove you home safely and would drop yer car off the next mornin'.

Come New Year's Eve there was a line of cars backed up from the gravel pit halfway into town. Local folks took to Hubert's place like pigs to a mud hole. The whole idea was a great success. Hubert made a fistful of money, the town was so quiet the cops practically had the night off, and Maine people got a chance to practice a grand old tradition with no harm done. Say what you like, I think Hubert done pretty good for such a numb kid.

Hubert Trains His Dog

When Hubert was growin' up, he always loved to play with other kids. Trouble was, other kids got tired of playin' with Hubert quite a bit sooner than he got tired of playin' with them.

Hubert always did have peculiar ideas about how things oughtta be done, which was apparent even back then when he kept comin' up with new rules for all the games kids have been playin' for years. 'Course the other kids didn't see nothin' wrong with the original rules, and that led to all kinds of problems.

For instance, when the other boys organized a baseball game, they'd set it up along traditional lines. They'd have a pitcher, a batter, two teams, outfielders, and so forth just like old Abner Doubleday designed it. The pitcher would throw the ball, the batter would swat at it, and the runners'd go around the bases in the reg'lar

order. Nobody had any complaints about the system.
Except Hubert.

When it come Hubie's turn to pitch, he figured it'd be
harder for the batter to hit the ball if the pitcher rolled it
like a bowlin' ball. Hubie was right, of course, in his own
weird way. Fact is, it was downright impossible to hit the
thing unless the batter swung at it like he had a golf club.
Hubert just figured that added excitement to the game.

The result of Hubert's tinkerin' with rules was that
anytime he was involved in a game, the whole thing
would grind to a halt and everybody would end up
bickerin' and not havin' any fun at all. So it wunt too
long before the other kids realized that any game they
was plannin' would go a whole lot smoother if Hubert
was somewhere else. He ended up spendin' more and
more time by himself. Mother and I got worried about
the boy bein' alone so much, and we decided maybe the
best thing would be to get him a pet.

41

One Saturday mornin' we all piled into the pickup and headed down to the Pittsfield animal shelter to get Hubert a dog. Everybody knows there's somethin' special about the relationship between a boy and his dog. But when the boy in question is our boy Hubert, the dog had better be somethin' pretty out of the ordinary if we expected it to take on the assignment.

When we got to the shelter there was all kinds of animals barkin', squawkin', and meowin' to beat the band, and the smell in that place would've embarrassed a skunk. We told the lady at the front desk we was lookin' to adopt a pet, and she ushered us in with the assurance they was all up for grabs.

Now nobody likes to mention the fact, but we all know what happens to them little puppies and kitties after they been at the shelter a couple of weeks. Hubert seemed to absorb this concept right off, and he made a beeline for the last row of pens where the most desperate cases waited just around the corner from you-know-where.

The minute I laid eyes on that pooch I knew we was in for an adventure. If there could ever be a canine version of Hubert, this critter was it. The dog was a mixture of several large breeds and a couple of small ones, which brought up uncomfortable images of the considerable gyrations that must of took place in order to bring that beast into existence.

It was love at first sight. That dog looked at Hubie like he'd found his long-lost pal, and Hubie returned the favor. I mean it. The very same look came across both their faces at the same moment. You might think it would be hard for a dog and a boy to get the same look on their faces at the same time, but I swear it's the truth.

HUBERT   SNOWBALL

As Mother and I signed the papers, Hubert lugged
the puppy out to the truck. I've never seen two livin'
creatures as happy as them two was at that moment.
Hubie had finally found the ideal playmate. The pair of
'em was livin', breathin' proof of the old adage "Ignorance
is bliss."

First thing Hubert had to do was come up with a
name for the pup. He finally settled on Snowball on
account of the color of the dog's fur, which was black,
brown, and white. I didn't even bother tryin' to figure
that one out. As long as Snowball didn't object, it was
OK by me.

After settlin' on a name, Hubert started trainin'
Snowball to do a few tricks. It was obvious right away
that Snowball shared Hubert's unique way of interpretin'
instructions. Hubert would pick up a stick, heave it off
into the puckerbrush, and yell "Fetch!" Snowball would
go boundin' off in hot pursuit, thrash around in the

43

bushes, and emerge at a gallop, tail waggin' and ears flappin', and deposit the prize in front of Hubert.

Only trouble was, whatever Snowball brought back bore no resemblance to the stick Hubert tossed out. Old hubcaps, antique medicine bottles, a generator from a 1949 Hudson Hornet, you name it, Snowball would find it and deposit it lovingly at his master's feet. Was Hubert upset? Not hardly. He understood the rules of the game as well as the dog did. With a pat on the head and a word of encouragement, Hubert would toss out another stick. No doubt about it, they was a perfect match.

Things went along pretty well for a couple of months. Then Hubert run across an ad in the back of an old *Mechanix Illustrated* magazine. That advertisement changed our lives forever. It was situated right smack-dab between "Can You Really Buy Surplus U.S. Army Jeeps for $44?" and "Finish Life at Home in Your Spare Time!" The ad had a picture of a German sheperd lookin' right atcha with a forlorn expression and a caption that read "Teach Your Dog to Talk!" It went on to say that for $19.95 they'd send you an audiocassette and phrase book guaranteed to teach any dog to talk in 30 days or your money back. Whoever wrote that ad must've had Hubert in mind.

Hubie turned in all his bottles, borrowed a couple dollars from Mother, filled out the mail-order coupon, and sent off for Snowball's correspondence course. About two weeks later it arrived by parcel post.

In the weeks that followed we hardly got a glimpse of Hubie and Snowball. For hours at a stretch they just stayed in the barn practicin' their lessons. Mother and I knew what was goin' on, but frankly we figured that as long as they was happy there was no harm done. That just goes to show how wrong you can be.

Almost a month to the day after that mail-order course arrived, Mother was havin' a few ladies from the church auxiliary over for afternoon tea. They was just takin' up the subject of food baskets for the starvin' kids in India when Hubert and Snowball burst into the den.

"Mama!" cried Hubert. "It worked! I taught him to talk, I really did!"

45

The ladies exchanged knowin' glances. They were all aware of Hubert's hare-brained projects, and their sympathy for Mother was evident.

"That's nice, dear," Mother said as casually as possible.

"No, I mean it." Hubie went on. "He can really talk. Wanna hear him?"

It was clear there was no way out. "Why I'm sure we'd all be delighted, wouldn't we, ladies?" Mother said with a note of urgency.

" 'Course, of course," the ladies indulgently replied.

The followin' demonstration took everybody by surprise. The church ladies was operatin' on the assumption that if Hubert had managed to teach his dog to talk, it would be along the traditional lines. Stuff like "What's that thing on top of the barn?" "Roof, roof." Or "How does sandpaper feel when you touch it?" "Ruff, ruff."

What they got instead was a lengthy monologue from Snowball on such absorbin' topics as effective methods of avoidin' flea bites, how to approach a postman when he's not lookin', and a truly movin' soliloquy on the grace and charm of the next-door neighbor's poodle, who happened to be in heat that month.

All in all, I'd have to say things worked out for the best. Mother's church group eventually got over the shock of the encounter, and Hubert learned a valuable lesson. Even if you succeed in teachin' yer dog to talk, you'll eventually have to face the fact that a dog just ain't got much to say!

Boneless Chicken

I hate to admit it, but once in awhile our boy Hubert can be pretty darn observant. 'Course he's constantly on the lookout for some new money-makin' scheme that'll drag in a wad of cash to bankroll the rest of his hare-brained ideas. And he gets his inspirations from some pretty unlikely places.

For instance, a while back we was out grocery shoppin' at Bud's Shop 'n Save in Newport. It was Friday night and folks had just got their paychecks, so the aisles was pretty well packed. As soon as we stepped in the door Hubert run right over and claimed his favorite shoppin' cart, the one with the right front wheel pointed off at a 45-degree angle. He never has to worry about someone else usin' it 'cause it's almost impossible to get the thing to go in a straight line. 'Course, realizing this, other customers put it back and pick another cart, but not

47

Hubie. He likes the challenge of tryin' to maneuver that rig around the store without hittin' somethin' every two minutes.

About halfway through our shoppin', Mother and I was in aisle 3, takin' advantage of a two-for-one sale on extra-large jars of Marshmallow Fluff, when I noticed Hubert was missin'. I figured we musta lost him in the last aisle, so I left Mother standin' there, turned around, and fought my way back through the crowd like salmon swimmin' upstream, jugglin' an armload of Marshmallow Fluff.

When I finally located Hubert he was gazin' into the meat freezer like it was a crystal ball. He didn't even look up when I spoke to him, but I could practically hear the gears whirrin' inside his skull, and I knew right off he was havin' one of his brainstorms. Believe me, anything serious goin' on inside that brain of Hubie's is likely to have more disasterous results than a full-blown nor'easter.

On the ride back home the boy hardly said a word. He just stared out the window mumblin' somethin' about boneless chicken and once in awhile scratchin' a few numbers on his little notepad. We'd no sooner pulled into the driveway than Hubert jumped outta the cab and took off for the barn with all the singlemindedness and blazin' speed of a bull moose in heat.

When Hubert latches onto an idea it really takes over his life. For the better part of three weeks Mother and I barely caught a glimpse of the boy. Except for the occasional disappearance of a couple of cans of Moxie or a whoopie pie from the icebox, Hubert could just as well have been livin' on Mars.

Just when we was beginnin' to wonder if we'd ever see him again, Hubert made his big announcement.

49

"Mother! Daddy!" he hollered, bangin' through the kitchen door just as we was settin' down to a plate of flapjacks. "You ain't gonna believe what I've just invented!"

"Prob'ly not," said Mother, settin' an extra place at the table. "Pull up a chair and have some breakfast, son. You must be half starved by now."

"But you don't understand what I'm sayin'," Hubert moaned.

"That's the God's honest truth," sighed Mother. "But I'm startin' to get used to it."

Hubert plunked himself down and between gulps of coffee and mouthfuls of flapjacks managed to explain that what he'd been inventin' out in the barn was boneless chicken. "I hate to break the news to you, boy," I said sympathetically, "but I'm afraid somebody got there ahead of y'. They've had boneless chicken down to the Shop 'n Save for quite awhile now."

"That's just where I got the idea, Daddy," Hubert went on excitedly. "Trouble with the boneless chicken they got down to the store is that it takes too much effort to get it that way."

Now Hubert has come up with some pretty strange projects over the years, but this one was bizarre even by his standards. The explanation that followed was classic Hubert logic. He'd figured from his investigations at the supermarket that folks was buyin' quite a load of that boneless chicken and that they was willin' to pay a premium price for it. Most of the high price tag on that chicken, he figured, was on account of the company havin' to pay folks to take the bones out first. That's where Hubert's invention come into the picture. He figured he could make a lot of money sellin' boneless

50

chicken if he could breed the critters without any bones
right from the git go. You prob'ly ain't gonna believe this,
but Hubert claimed that's exactly what he'd been workin'
on for the past few weeks. The first batch of chicks was
due to hatch out over the weekend.

When the big event come it was more or less the
same as any batch of chicks hatchin' out. They pecked
their way through the shells and flopped around tryin' to
get their bearin's for a minute or two. The primary difference between normal chicks and this new breed of
Hubie's was that instead of hoppin' up and pokin' around
like you'd expect newborn chicks to do, they just kinda
layed there on the straw 'til they dried off and fluffed up.
They didn't seem the least bit unhappy, you understand.
They was chirpin' away to beat the band, but it was
obvious from the outset that there wunt a single bone
amongst 'em.

51

Hubert was ecstatic. The whole experiment was goin' along accordin' to schedule. He'd already figured out that them little boneless chicks would need a certain amount of special care to keep 'em healthy and happy, and he was ready to accommodate 'em. In anticipation of the blessed event, he'd collected several dozen pairs of worn-out panty hose. Just where he found 'em I can't rightly say, and frankly I feel a whole lot more comfortable not knowin'. But somehow he got ahold of 'em, cut out the feet, and tacked 'em up in neat little rows on the walls of the barn.

Hubert explained that since the chicks were born without bones they couldn't very well be expected to set up in the nest like ordinary chicks. For instance, if they was to flop over in the night they might smother themselves. So he had devised a special handlin' procedure. One by one he picked up them cute little newborn boneless chicks and dropped 'em into their own little panty-hose nest. The idea was that no mattter how much they flopped around, they'd always be able to breath through the nylon. I'll admit it looked strange, but it *was* clever in a Hubert sort of way.

The success of Hubie's boneless chicken business was phenomenal. Word of his groundbreakin' genetic engineerin' experiment spread all over the county, and before long the press got wind of it. It wunt unusual to look out the kitchen window and see two or three TV camera crews pullin' into the yard at one time.

Meanwhile them chicks was growin' up fast, developin' into fine lookin' boneless hens and roosters right before our eyes. 'Course they never really got the knack of flyin', or even walkin' for that matter. They just sorta hung out in the barnyard sun lookin' like little

52

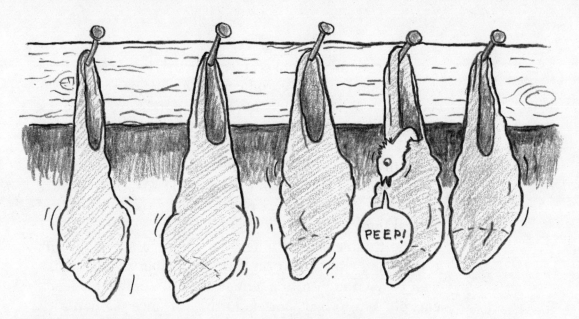

PEEP!

feathered Nerf balls. Whenever one of them TV vans come screechin' into the yard, them chickens'd blow around in the wake of it like so many dandelion pods in the breeze. All in all, I must say they seemed to be enjoyin' themselves.

It's not very often that one of Hubert's schemes turns out as good as the boneless chicken project. It's prob'ly just as well because when he *does* get somethin' right it just encourages him. The boneless chicken business was a prime example of a situation where Hubie shoulda quit while he was ahead. He was makin' out just fine 'til he decided to expand his horizons.

Hubie figured if his technique worked on chickens it might have other commercial applications. Since boneless ham was also a popular item, Hubert decided to try his hand at growin' a crop of boneless pigs. To give him credit, I have to say the early results was encouragin'. But as anybody who's been around a farm can tell you, there's a lot more involved in raisin' hogs than raisin' chickens, the primary issue bein' the size of the animal.

53

As I say, things looked OK at first. There's few critters on God's green earth could compare with them little newborn boneless piglets for sheer adorability. They was cute and pink and docile as lambs. On chilly fall mornin's I'd pick one up and drape it around my neck like a scarf. The little fella would lay right there all mornin' long as I went about my chores, and from the look on his face I'd say he was as happy as a pig in...well, you get the general idea.

The trouble started when them boneless hogs begun to get some real weight on 'em. Up to that point it had been easy enough to lug 'em around the barnyard, feed 'em, put 'em to bed, and so forth. But once we had a couple dozen of them critters approachin' 300 pounds each, all the fun seemed to evaporate outta the endeavor. First thing we had to do was hire on a whole new crew to tend them hogs, which just about eliminated any profit margin we mighta been lookin' at. Plus it wunt easy to find men willin' to do that sorta work on a daily basis.

Since them hogs was pretty much unable to get around on their own, the hired hands had to work from sunup 'til sundown usin' crowbars, two-by-fours, and anything else they could get their hands on to roll them critters from the barn to the pasture and back again. That was bad enough in itself, but if it happened to be a hot day, the hogs needed to be turned every hour or so or else they'd get sunburned.

I could keep on goin', but I think you get the general idea. Hubert's dreams of fame and fortune evaporated like the steam risin' offa them boneless pigs in the heat of the midday sun. Was he discouraged? Not hardly. A lot of folks would set back and lick their wounds after an episode like that, but not Hubert. He was out in the barn

bright and early the next mornin' workin' on a new
genetic hybrid. He claims he's got secret information
that'll lead to the development of a new strain of gasless
beans. That'd really revolutionize Saturday night church
suppers! I can't wait to try 'em.

55

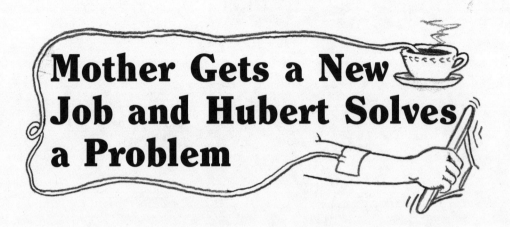

Mother Gets a New Job and Hubert Solves a Problem

I honestly don't know how we'd get by around here without Mother. Besides bein' a good wife and a good mother, she's just about always held down at least one outside job to supplement the family income. Like a lot of Maine women, she started workin' early in life and she ain't slowed down a mite since. Matter of fact, Mother was barely 12 years old when she got her first payin' job, workin' durin' summer vacations as a runner down to Robbie Robinson's Used Auto Parts in Clinton. Robbie or one of his boys would pick her up at the crack o' dawn, and she'd put in a full eight-hour day, six days a week. Mother was the best runner goin', and she kept that summer job right through high school.

A lot of years has gone by since then, and Mother's always worked hard at a whole raft of different jobs to help make ends meet. Some of 'em was better than

others, but I never really worried about her too much 'cause she never took a job I thought was dangerous. That is, up until about two years ago when she took a job drivin' a truck.

It's a generic beer truck. You prob'ly seen one of 'em out on the turnpike a few times. Big white truck with black letters across the side of it, just says BEER. Matter of fact, it just says TRUCK across the front. That's on accounta it's operated by that generic company. Mother gets a check from 'em every two weeks just like clockwork. It's a plain white check with black letters up in the left-hand corner, just says THE COMPANY. I imagine you've seen their products down to the supermarket. There'll be a can on the shelf, white can, black letters, just says SOUP on the label. It don't tell y' what kind. Just SOUP. 'Course the prices are cheaper than the name-brand stuff, so a lotta folks take a chance on 'em. Far as I can see, this stuff is gettin' so popular that eventually you'll walk into the store and see whole shelves lined with cans and boxes, all different shapes and sizes, every one of 'em white with black letters that just says FOOD.

Since she's been with the company, Mother has earned a few premiums for her hard work and dedication. One of my favorites was a set of matchin' his 'n her generic sweatshirts. They're white with black letters across the front that just say CONSUMER with them little lines and numbers across the bottom. The idea is that when you do yer shoppin' at one of them new places with the automatic beeper at the cash register, you go through the line, pay the cashier, then lay down across the little beep window on the counter. That way they'll know you been there.

Another nice item Mother got from the company was somethin' they claim is the latest literary trend, the generic novel. You ever seen one of 'em? I can tell you it's a great gift idea for folks like me. I've always been a reader, but I'll admit I've never really gone in for that heavy literature stuff. I mostly prefer somethin' light, like the back side of a Comet can or maybe a box of corn-flakes; somethin' you can get through in one settin'.

That generic novel was ideal readin'. It was a paper-back, only about 100 pages, so not too intimidatin'. The cover was white with black letters that just said BOOK. Once I started readin', I just couldn't put it down. It was

a story about this fella (didn't mention exactly who) who
lived in this town (no particular name to the town either).
I tell y', I appreciate a book like that. It was a darn good
story, but it didn't bog y' down with a lot of details.

Anyway, to get back to my story. Truck drivin' can be
real dangerous, especially in rural Maine in the winter-
time. Long hours, icy roads, 10-year-old kids on
snowmobiles bashin' across the roads all hours of the day
and night. Not that Mother ain't a careful driver. But I
worry just the same, 'specially when she has to drive a
lot of hours without gettin' much sleep.

'Course Mother always carries a thermos of hot black
coffee with her on them long hauls. Mother and I both
love our coffee, but not that whimpy brew you see adver-

59

tised on TV. No sir, I guess that stuff'd be all right if you dumped a handful of No-Doz in each cup, but when we drink coffee we're lookin' for caffeine and lots of it. And that's just where the trouble come in with this truck drivin' business. As long as Mother gets plenty of caffeine into 'er on them trips, I don't worry. But that process ain't necessarily as easy as it sounds.

If you've ever tried to drive one of them big rigs on an icy back road at 3:00 in the mornin' while jugglin' a hot cup of java, you know what I'm gettin' at. It's all well and good to lug the stuff around on the seat next to you. But tryin' to get it poured into the cup and from the cup into yer mouth without goin' off the road is another matter.

I finally got so nervous about the whole situation that I mentioned it to our boy Hubert after supper one night. He listened to everythin' I had to say, and by the time I got done I could tell he was pretty concerned, too. "Well, son," I said when I got done, "thanks for hearin' me out, but I don't want you to worry too much. The way I see it, there ain't a thing we can do about it anyways."

Thinkin' back on it, I realize I shoulda knowed better. As I was talkin' I could just about hear the gears whirrin' inside of Hubie's brain. By the time I got through, he had a look on his face like some possessed critter in a Stephen King movie. "I'll be back in a minute," he mumbled. "I think I got me an idea."

Next thing I knew, Hubert shot straight out the door makin' a beeline for that workshop of his in the barn. Now when Hubert gets the inspiration for a new invention, there's two things that's always true. First off, whatever the idea is you can bet it ain't never so much as entered the mind of another human bein'. Second, once he gets goin' on it he won't quit 'til he's got it done. In this case the project took him about three days.

Meantime, Mother had made it safely back from another trip and was enjoyin' several days off before she had to go back on the road again. I'd almost forgotten my discussion with Hubert when he burst breathlessly into the parlor on Sunday afternoon and proudly announced, "Mother, Daddy, it's done!"

Startled by the sudden outburst, Mother and I looked up from the Sunday paper. "What's done?" we replied in unison.

"It's a surprise," Hubert said excitedly. "You gotta come outside to see it."

Over the years we've learned that when Hubert's in a mood like this, the quickest route back to normalcy is to go along with him. Reluctantly we got on our boots, coats, and mittens and stepped out into the winter chill. Hubie was jumpin' around the driveway like fat on a griddle.

"Over here!" he yelled, pointin' at the cab of Mother's truck, which was parked at the far end of the drive. As we approached the cab, I noticed somethin' weird hangin' off the driver's side rearview mirror that definitely wunt there when Mother pulled in a couple days earlier. "That's it!" squealed Hubie triumphantly. "My new invention!"

We stared at the contraption for a minute or two, and finally Mother found her voice. "It's very nice, son," she said kindly, "but what is it?"

"First of its kind in the world!" Hubert crowed. "Specially designed for long-haul truckers! I call it the Mr. Coffee I-V Unit!" While we looked on helplessly, Hubert proceeded to demonstrate how it worked.

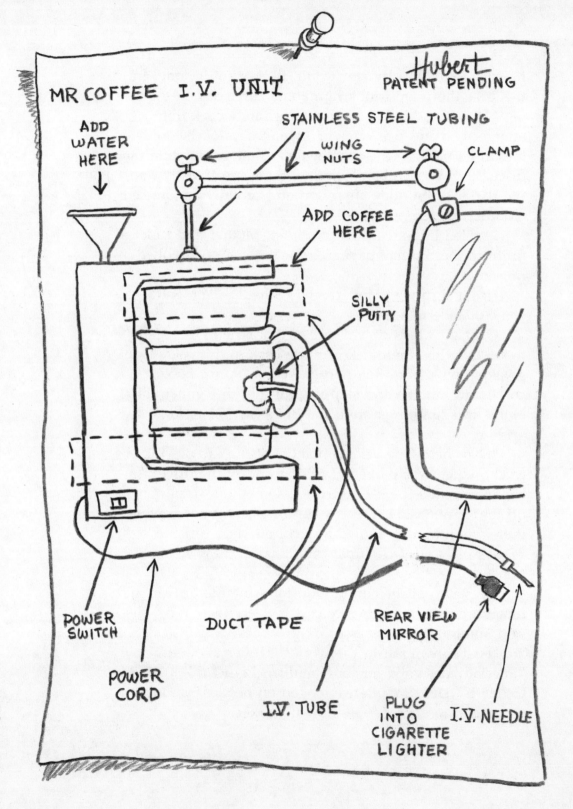

Hangin' off the mirror on the driver's side of the truck was most of what used to be a regular automatic-drip coffee maker. It was a big one, I'd say maybe a 12- to 14-cup job. It was modified with a hanger on the top and counterweights on the bottom to keep it steady under adverse road conditions, and there was what looked like two small wires runnin' from the bottom of the coffee maker into a small hole Hubert had drilled in the vent window. He'd even plugged the hole with Silly Putty to keep out the draft and prevent chaffin'. "Now, Mother, just climb into the cab and I'll show you how it works," said Hubie.

Mother followed Hubie's instructions. I jumped in alongside her, and Hubert climbed in next to me. Once we was inside we could see that instead of two wires there was only one. That was the cord that ran directly into the cigarette lighter to provide power to the unit. The other thing we thought was a cord was actually a small piece of plastic tubin' that Hubert had somehow acquired from an I-V unit down to the Pittsfield health clinic. When it comes to Hubie's inventions, you learn not to ask too many questions.

The biggest surprise of all come when he explained how the thing worked. What I mean is, the danged thing actually worked! What happens is this. You plug the power cord into the cigarette lighter, and before you know it the unit outside yer window starts perkin' away with fresh hot coffee. When that happens, you just plug that I-V tube right into yer left arm. It takes a little gettin' used to, but once you get the hang of it, it's pretty easy. Hubie even supplied a roll of duct tape to hold the tube in place.

Now I've never seen anything like that invention.
Since Hubert installed his Mr. Coffee I-V Unit on Mother's
truck, she can run all day and night with a constant
supply of fresh-brewed coffee and both hands firmly
planted on the steerin' wheel. With all that caffeine
runnin' through her, she's prob'ly jacked up like an old
barn, but I'm sleepin' better 'n I have in years.

Snappy Answers

Snappy Answers

One thing Mainers have always been famous for is the way we have of respondin' to the swarm of questions put to us by outsiders. When confronted with a question from someone who's obviously from away, a native downeaster is apt to reply with a snappy one-liner that not only answers the question but places the whole conversation in a different perspective. My Uncle Steve, who runs a little store on the way into Eastport, Maine, is a longtime practitioner of this Yankee art form.

Even before he opened up his corner store, Unc had a small farm on the same property, and pretty reg'lar he'd get questioned by passersby on any number of topics. One mornin' he was up about 5:30 replacin' a few rotted-out fence posts where his pasture bordered the main road. As he made his way across the meadow he noticed a lone figure standin' along the roadside next to one of

67

them little English sports cars. A young fella was decked out just like he was goin' on safari, complete with a half dozen or so cameras slung around his neck.

Unc paid him no mind and went about diggin postholes with the cameras clickin' and whirrin' in the background. After about a half hour, that young fella had apparently got whatever he was after. He packed up his gear, jumped into the car, and fired her up. Just when Unc figured he was gonna be left to himself, the car screeched to a halt.

The driver jumped out, clearin' the ditch in one leap, and breathless with excitement, run right up to Unc. "Excuse me, sir," he blurted out.

"Why, what'd you do?" says Unc.

"No, I mean, I don't want to bother you."

"Takes a lot more'n this to bother me, son," Unc replied.

"Well," the young fella went on, "it's just that I've been photographing your wildlife this morning, and there's something I don't understand. Maybe you could explain it to me."

"More'n likely I could," says Unc, "only first you got to ask me the question."

"Well, I've been noticing that some of these cows I was photographing, like that one over there, for instance, have horns and some don't. I just wondered if you could explain why that is."

Unc set down the maul he'd been usin' and took out his pipe and got it goin', takin' his time and starin' at a patch of sky just above the young fella's forehead. When he got the pipe goin', he replied.

"Now that's a good question, son. Lot of folks wouldn't be clever enough to come up with a question

68

smart as that. Fact is, there's a lot of different reasons
why you might see a cow without horns. For one thing,
every now and then we get a cow that's kind of rambunc-
tious, stavin' up the stalls and so forth, so we gotta cut
the horns off 'em. Then there's a chance a cow 'll bust
through this here fencin' and ram around the woods and
knock a horn off on a stump or a rock or somethin'. On
top o' that we got them foreign-bred cows nowadays.
They breed them critters overseas someplace an' darned if
they don't breed the horns right out of 'em altogether. But

69

if you're referrin' to that particular animal you was pointin' to a minute ago, the reason that one ain't got no
horns is...that's a horse."

70

A few years after that incident, Unc built his store right on that same corner, and it seemed like every outta-stater that stopped in for a cup of coffee or a six-pack of beer and some Slim Jims had at least one question. Unc was always ready with an appropriate response.

"How far is it from here to Portland?" one tourist asked.

"I'd say about 3,000 miles," replied Unc, "the way you're headed."

One Sunday afternoon a young couple pulled up to the gas pumps out front in one of them miniature cars that's so popular these days, the kind that gets 50 miles to the gallon only you're so scrunched up inside that a 50-mile trip would darn near kill y'. As he was pumpin' the gas, the young fella glanced over at Unc's '64 Pontiac Bonneville. At several tons, that Pontiac is the pinnacle of the time-honored Detroit tradition of "road-huggin' weight."

Aimin' his question at Unc, who was settin' in his rockin' chair out front of the store, the young fella sneered, "Why on earth would anybody drive a gas-guzzler like that these days? I'll bet it doesn't get 10 miles to the gallon."

"Matter of fact, on a good day it only gets about eight," Unc replied. "On the other hand, I ain't particularly worried about mileage. I already live here."

One fall I was helpin' Unc out around the store in the evenin's. It was deer huntin' season, and we was doin' a land-office business. I was just about to pull the plug on the Pabst Blue Ribbon beer sign about 11:00 when this big pickup lurches off the highway and pulls up right in front of the store.

I give Unc a quick glance. He was tired and a mite cranky, but he patted the top of the cash register to indicate we was still open for business. There was four hunters in that truck, and from the hootin', hollerin', and stumblin' around that accompanied their exit from the cab, I knew it was the Pabst Blue Ribbon sign that had attracted 'em.

Unc walked over to the front window to check out the situation. The truck was a big ol' three-quarter-ton Ford 4x4 with a fiberglass cap and New York plates, and it was loaded down worse than a Canadian pulp truck. There was three or four good-sized deer strapped onto the fenders, a couple of Christmas trees on the roof rack, and a whole assortment of junk loaded top to bottom on the back. They had everything from driftwood to lobster traps, maple syrup, and souvenier ashtrays. It's a wonder the tires didn't blow out with the weight of that rollin' flea market.

By the time they sorted themselves out an' made it in the front door Unc was back behind the cash register, eager to make the last sale of the day. It was obvious he'd made the right move in stayin' open a few extra minutes.

The crew went about their shoppin' with a vengeance. The way they stripped the shelves put me in mind of one of them TV game shows where you win a shoppin' spree for a few minutes at some supermarket. It only took 'em about five minutes, but by the time Unc had rung up their haul, they'd darn near cleaned us out of everything from beer and cigarettes to Playboy air-fresheners and Octagon soap.

After paying cash money for all this booty (more money in five minutes than Unc had prob'ly seen in a week), the driver leaned over the counter and addressed

a question to Unc. "I need a bit of advice."

"What seems to be the problem?" says Unc.

"Well," the driver replied, "we're apt to be drivin' all night, and I was just wonderin', can we take this road all the way back to New York?"

Unc paused a moment, glanced out the window at that overloaded pickup, then back at the four customers luggin' off most of his inventory into the night. "You might as well," he muttered. "Looks like y' already got about everything else."

I don't wanna give you the impression that Unc has some kinda monopoly on one-liners. One of the all-time champions in the Maine Snappy Answers Hall of Fame

73

lives down to Rockland. His given name is Edward L. Hutchinson, but to everyone in Knox County he's just plain "Hutch."

Hutch is a dyed-in-the-wool native with roots in the Rockland area that go back about 10 generations. Every one of them generations has eked out a livin' same as Hutch does, fishin'. Last summer, for the first time in years, Hutch spent nearly a whole week ashore. For a deepwater man like him, that had to be an all-time record. But you'll have to admit he had a darned good excuse.

One Monday afternoon last August, Hutch stopped by Goodnow's Pharmacy on Main Street in Rockland. Regular as clockwork every day for years, Hutch has stopped by the pharmacy after the catch is in for a cup of coffee, a half hour or so of local gossip, and the latest edition of the *Camden Herald*. Everything went as usual that day last August, except that when Hutch plunked down at the counter and glanced at the paper, he found he was front-page news.

The headline story said that a local gentleman, Edward L. Hutchinson, was one of three individuals who would share the jackpot in the Tri-State Megabucks lottery. More'n six million dollars would be divided equally between Hutchinson, a real estate salesman from Keene, New Hampshire, and a young lady restaurateur from Portland. You might think it odd nobody broke the news to Hutch before he read it for himself, but you got to remember that none of the regulars at Goodnow's had any idea that Edward L. Hutchinson was the fisherman settin' right next to 'em. If they'da had any idea, there's prob'ly several five- and ten-dollar markers that woulda been called due on the spot.

Word got out fast. By the time Hutch pulled into his driveway, the press was waitin' out in front of his trailer. Hutch was already confused enough as it was, and a flock of reporters hollerin' at him and stickin' microphones in his face didn't help. He shooed 'em away as polite as he could with a mumbled promise to talk to 'em later after he'd had a chance to think a mite.

For the rest of the week Hutch did somethin' he hadn't done in years. He just stayed home. He didn't go fishin'. He didn't stop in to Goodnow's. He just stayed home with the phone off the hook and the door bolted

75

and tried to ponder out the implications of this turn of events. About midweek he got notified by mail that the lottery commissioner was invitin' him and the other two winners to a presentin' ceremony at the Sonesta Hotel ballroom down to Portland. The letter said Hutch'd get a check (for more money than he thought existed in the whole damned country), plus he'd be asked to answer a few questions from the press. Hutch wunt too thrilled with the part about answerin' questions, but he figured he oughtta at least go pick up the danged check.

On the big day Hutch pulled up in front of the hotel right on schedule. A young fella in some kinda costume convinced him to part with the keys to his pickup and drove off to park it in the hotel lot. Hutch stepped into the buildin', nervously awaitin' his appointment. The aroma that trailed in his wake was a curious mixture consistin' of roughly equal parts Old Spice, Old GrandDad, and old fish.

At the ballroom, the lottery commissioner himself met Hutch at the door, pumped his hand enthusiastically, and led him up to the stage where the other two winners were already seated. The place was jam-packed, and TV cameras from all the local stations was crankin' away at full throttle. Hutch was about as comfortable as the town drunk at a revival meetin'.

He did his best to set still through the preliminaries, and when they called his name he come forward amidst the cheerin' crowd, pumped the commissioner's hand again, grinned so hard he thought his dentures would crack, muckled onto that check, and made his way back to his seat half-blinded by flash bulbs and TV lights.

When the official ceremony was over, the crowd thinned out and the TV crews converged on the winners.

Basically they had one question, "What are you going to
do with all this money?"

The young restaurant owner spoke first. Drawlin' in a
thick southern accent that instantly pegged her as bein'
from away, she said she planned to add a new dining
room to her establishment on the waterfront. The New
Hampshire real estate fella said he intended to invest his
millions in luxury condominiums nestled in the splendor
of the White Mountains.

Hutch was busy studyin' the pattern of water marks
on his old leather work boots when the reporters finally

turned on him. Even though *he* was nervous, the folks watchin' the proceedin's on the tube back in Rockland knew Hutch had earned his reputation for snappy one-liners. They knew he wouldn't let 'em down even under all that pressure, and by God he didn't.

The first reporter to nail Hutch was Russ Van Arsdale, that nice young fella from the Bangor station who'd come all the way to Portland for the inside scoop. "Mr. Hutchinson," he asked, "all our viewers are anxious to know what an authentic Maine fisherman like yourself would possibly do with more than two million dollars."

"Well," says Hutch, starin' straight at the camera and all the folks at home, "I'll prob'ly just keep on fishin' 'til it's all gone!"

The Mary Kay Girl

The Mary Kay Girl

One of my favorite neighbors is Marlene, the Mary Kay girl. If you've never heard tell of that Mary Kay stuff, you've missed quite a lot. What it is, you see, is a whole raft of fancy cosmetics that women sell door-to-door to their former friends and so forth. One of the best parts of doin' Mary Kay is that after a woman sells a couple of tons of them cosmetics, the company gives her a free car. That's hard to believe, I know, but it's the God's honest truth. I've seen it with my own eyes.

Now some of the fellas around here ain't too keen on that Mary Kay. Matter of fact, there's a few of 'em that's dead set against it on the grounds it keeps their women-folk out rammin' the roads at ungodly hours, sometimes as late as 7:30 or 8:00 at night. Personally, though, I have to say I've got nothin' whatsoever against them cosmetics. Matter of fact, they've made quite a few ladies out our way considerably easier to look at.

83

Marlene, of course, is a real charmer in her own right. Personality plus, that's what she is. And wicked cunnin', too. Even before she took up sellin' that Mary Kay, I had her pegged as a real fine specimen of feminine pulchritude.

First off, Marlene's got one thing goin' for her that most Maine men find darn near irresistible. She's a real good heavyset girl. I can't for the life of me see the attraction in them skinny girls you see on the covers of the glossy magazines at the checkout counter down to the supermarket. You know the type I'm referrin' to. They slouch around with a pout on their face like their dog just got run over. They're skinny as a rail fence, with their cheeks all caved in. And likely as not, they're only half dressed. Godfrey mighty! A girl built like that wouldn't make it halfway through a Maine winter. Sure, a fella might be tempted to gawk at them girls when he's buyin' this week's Megabucks ticket. But when it comes to warmth and comfort durin' a three-day blizzard, nothin' can compare with sheer physical bulk. Without strainin' the truth, I'd say Marlene'd dress out at 275 pounds or better.

About a year after she started sellin' them cosmetics, Marlene pulled up in front of our trailer in a great big pink Buick. She'd earned her free car. It weren't exactly spankin' new, but it was mighty slick lookin' all the same. Power everything on that baby. That front seat was as big and squishy as any sofa I ever set on. It had a power ashtray that'd practically jump onto your lap at the flip of a switch and even a power antenna. 'Course the antenna just had a bent coat hanger stuck in the socket, but it went up and down just the same. Marlene had the Whipple boys over to Newport chop off the body just behind the driver's seat and had a plywood flatbed built onto the hind end.

Say what you want, but one thing's for sure, you can haul a wicked load of cosmetics around on that rig. You go ahead and laugh all you want, but when Marlene pulls into the gravel pit on a Saturday night in that rig, she's *somebody*. The only complaint she's ever had about that car is that it came off the lot with one of them FM stereo radios, and she was a little peeved at havin' to order an AM converter in order to pick up the good stations.

Ayuh, I'd say Marlene definitely has a sense of style that's pretty hard to ignore. You take that little pooch of hers. Most folks out our way 'll settle for a mess of beagles tied up out back or a couple of mutts lounging on

85

the tailgate of the pickup. But not Marlene, no sirree Bob. She's got her some real class. When she first got that job sellin' Mary Kay she hightailed it all the way up to Bangor and got her one of them fancy French "puddle" dogs. She claims they originally come from all the way over to France. Don't look a bit like a puddle in my book, but it does bear a pretty strong resemblance to a piece of fancy-cut shrubbery strainin' out at the end of that leash.

Now I got to admit I owe Marlene a personal debt. A couple of months back she invited Mother to one of them Mary Kay parties. You got to understand that them parties are one of the main ways them Mary Kay girls pump up the local clientele. They invite the ladies over for a free demonstration of their fine line of cosmetics, and when the party's over they send 'em on home with a free starter-kit of some hot-sellin' items. This is to sorta prime the pump for future sales. The idea is to get the new girls so fired up about the free samples that they'll join right up and start pushin' the stuff on their own.

Well, it just happens that on the very evenin' Marlene invited Mother out to that party, I'd made plans to spend the night out myself. It was league bowlin' night at Elsie's Candlepin Lanes down next to the laundromat. But come to find out Dewey Langley, best man on the team, had turned his ankle somethin' wicked tryin' to drop-kick a raccoon that had gotton into his trash can, and we ended up with a forfeit.

So that's how I happened to be home early when Mother got in from that Mary Kay party. She come a-bargin' through the door all in a tizzy on accounta missin' the first few minutes of Lawrence Welk, plopped them cosmetics on the kitchen table, and made a beeline for the sofa. She was so all fired wound up about that TV show she never even noticed me settin' there at ten past eight in the evenin'. On league bowlin' night!

Once Mother was settled in the livin' room, I took a gander at the package she'd flopped down on the kitchen table. Darned if it wunt one of them free sample packs of Mary Kay stuff. There was powders, perfumes, nail polish, and just all manner of refurbishin' hardware designed to enhance the feminine mystique.

One item in particular just seemed to catch my eye. It was a pretty good size tube of lipstick, and (you can believe this or not, but it's true) it was the *exact same* color as that safety orange the deer hunters wear. I'm not kiddin'. You know what color I'm talkin' about. That special orange stuff that jumps out atcha. You see it all the time durin' huntin' season. Or in the off-season it's the same color the road crews and them flagpersons use while they're tyin' up Route One all summer long. Well, I'll be darned if it wunt the same color stickin' outta that lipstick tube.

Now say what you want about folks sellin' cosmetics door-to-door, but soon as I saw that lipstick my mind was set. All I can tell y' is I knew right then and there I'd feel safer ridin' in the car at night with Mother if she was wearin' that lipstick.

I figure it this way. What if we happen to be drivin' along a dirt road late at night and we get a flat or run out of gas or somethin'? Why, all Mother'll have to do is step out onto the shoulder and pucker up a few times at reg'lar intervals, and we'll have a cop there in no time.

The Teeth

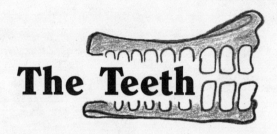

The Teeth

One of the luxuries of livin' in Maine is that you can still find a pretty decent selection of diners up here. In case you ain't been payin' attention, it's my sad duty to inform you that the good ol' owner-operated, fryolator-scented, greasy spoon American diner is without a doubt on the Endangered Species list. Diners are a vanishin' breed all over the country these days, but here in the Pine Tree State, I'm happy to report there's still quite a few of 'em open for business.

I don't mean to imply them fast-food joints ain't made some significant inroads. They're here, all right. All you got to do is cruise up Route One, and you'll find plenty of places loadin' folks up with an exact replica of what they're dishin' out from Timbuktu to Kalamazoo, along with enough paper goods and styrofoam to start your own bonfire.

91

'Course it's more'n just the food they serve that makes diners special. It's the whole feel of the places. Each and every diner in Maine is an orig'nal enterprise. Lots of 'em have been run by the same family for generations, which is more'n you can say for them plastic burger palaces. You don't believe me? Next time you stroll through the golden arches, ask to speak with Mr. McDonald. He don't even exist! And although Roy Rogers is a real live person, you're not apt to find him hangin' out at one of his restaurants either. See what I mean?

On the other hand, if you was to stop by Moody's Diner some afternoon and ask to have a word with Percy Moody, you'd see right off that you was in a whole different ballpark. I ain't promisin' he'd give you an audience, but if you caught him in the right mood he might. The whole point is, there's just a different way of doin' things at a diner. If you've never tried it, you don't know what you're missin'.

At a diner things are different from the minute you walk in the door. First off, diners specialize in that homey lived-in look. Instead of hard plastic seats and bare, antiseptic walls that remind you of the waitin' room at the vet's, you're more likely to find a row of booths with soft, padded seats decked out with swatches of duct tape where the rips are. The counter is usually yellow or pastel green linoleum with cigarette burns on the top, old bubble gum underneath, and a worn, scalloped edge where a couple of generations of truck drivers have rested their elbows.

In a good diner, the owner is prob'ly somewhere out back. You can see the cook and the dishwasher through the skinny little window they pass the food through. The waitresses tend to be plump and friendly with names like Shirley and Elsa. And a diner is one of the few places left on earth where you can still find a professional waitress. I'm not talkin' about high school and college kids lookin' for part-time work or retirees supplementin' their social security. I'm talkin' about honest-to-goodness, been-here-35-years, veteran hash slingers. Walk into a really good diner, plunk yerself down, and ask the waitress what they've got for dessert. Without so much as pausin' for a gulp of air, she'll rattle off 15 or 20 items, all the way from chocolate cream pie to homemade tapioca puddin'. Right then and there you'll know you're dealin' with a pro.

One of our favorite diners ain't really a diner at all. It's a truck stop, but it's got all the ingredients of a great restaurant in the finest diner tradition. To start with, it's been there forever, the kinda place where folks bring their grandkids to set at the same booth they used to set at when they was young. The place I'm referrin' to is just south of Bangor, right off Route 95. You can tell when you're close because the big rigs swarm around the place like hornets on an over-ripe peach.

When you pull into the parkin' lot you'll notice somethin' different right away. Stretched out in long rows are about 35 or 40 gas pumps. Just downwind of the pumps is the restaurant. To make sure you don't miss the convenience of all them pumps, they have a tall sign that says "Dysart's Truck Stop. Eat here, get gas!"

Since most of the regular customers at Dysart's are truck drivers, the place is designed to make 'em comfortable. Some folks might get nervous eatin' a chicken-salad sandwich next to an almost lifesize paintin' of an 18-wheel Kenworth Diesel headed straight at 'em, but it makes them truckers feel right to home. Over to the gift shop area are the necessities of long-haul truckin'. There's a good supply of tapes by such legendary artists as Boxcar Willy, Slim Whitman, and Utah Phillips, and Dysart's is one of the few outlets nationwide where you can still get the original version of Dusty Rhodes's country classic "If Ya Wanna Keep the Six-Pack Cold, Put it Next to My Ex-Wife's Heart" on eight-track cassette.

One Wednesday evenin' Mother and I decided to stop in to Dysart's around suppertime for some of their famous homemade chicken potpie. We were just settlin' into our booth when we noticed an elderly couple takin' their seats across the way from us. They both musta been 90 if they was a day, but from all the grinnin' and holdin' hands and so forth you'da thought they was a couple of school kids out on their first date.

He hung up her coat and helped her into her seat. Then he took out a little candle, lit it, and planted it in the truck-tire ashtray between 'em. We couldn't help glan-

cin' at 'em. As I watched, I thought I remembered Paul
Harvey sayin' on the radio that afternoon that a couple
from Bangor, Maine, had won the Tournament of Roses.
That's Mr. Harvey's way of honorin' the couple that's been
married the longest of anybody in the whole country. I

leaned over and mentioned it to Mother, and she agreed they was prob'ly the very couple we'd heard about. Now generally we wouldn't be so nosey, but with such big celebrities settin' right next to us, we paid mightly close attention to what was goin' on.

They ordered a large bottle of Moxie and two glasses. After the waitress brought 'em, the man offered a toast. "I told ya so," I whispered across the table to Mother. "It's got to be them!" When the waitress returned, the man ordered two "Big Rigs," one for each of 'em. The Big Rig is Dysart's top-of-the-line entree, a great gigantic hunk of flame-broiled steak smothered in mushrooms and onions. I wouldn't order one unless you're real hungry.

Them two lovebirds went on cooin', holdin' hands, and gazin' into each others eyes right up 'til the meal arrived. That's when Mother and I noticed a curious thing. As soon as their dinner was laid out on the table, that old lady attacked it like a pit bull terrier. Knife and fork flyin', she dove into that beef like she was starvin' to death. Strangely enough, though, while she was flailin' away, her husband just set there grinnin' at her. I mean to say he never so much as picked up his fork.

The whole scene looked pretty odd. We didn't mean to stare, but they really did make quite a spectacle. After a few minutes, the waitress finally caught on and walked over to their booth. We couldn't help overhearin' the conversation.

"Well now," the waitress said. "How's everything goin' over here?"

"Oh, just fine," the man replied. "Couldn't be better."

"I just wondered," the waitress shot back, "if there was anything wrong with yer meal. I noticed yer wife here seems to be enjoyin' hers, but you haven't touched a

bite all evenin'. What seems to be the problem?"

Suddenly the old gentleman begun to look pale as a ghost. He didn't say anything, but in a few seconds his color changed again. This time he was blushin' like a beet. The waitress saw he was embarrassed and jumped in to bail him out. "I didn't mean to upset y', sir," she said. "I just wanted to make sure the meal was done to yer likin'."

Regainin' his composure, the old man turned to the waitress, gave her a little wink, cupped his hands, and whispered, "No, no, dear, nothin' wrong with the food at all. I'm just waitin' for Mother to get through with the teeth."

97